Original title:
Life: It's All Part of the Plan… Maybe

Copyright © 2025 Creative Arts Management OÜ
All rights reserved.

Author: Jude Lancaster
ISBN HARDBACK: 978-1-80566-203-7
ISBN PAPERBACK: 978-1-80566-498-7

Mosaic of Moments

A splash of green upon my plate,
A coffee break that can't be late.
The cat thinks he's the boss today,
While I just grin, and just obey.

A dance with socks that don't quite match,
A tumble down, a perfect catch.
The phone rings twice, I chase the sound,
Yet trip on dreams that hug the ground.

The Balance of Chaos

My car's engine grumbles, what a fuss,
But I just let it ride the bus.
The toast is burnt, it's not a crime,
I'll blame it on too much time.

A toddler's tantrum out of sight,
Turns chaos into pure delight.
The dog steals socks, that's his grand plan,
And I just roll with what I can.

Navigating Through Shadows

Life's a maze of socks and keys,
I trip on shadows, please, oh please.
A late-night snack, a spoonful loud,
I hope the fridge won't call a crowd.

Directions on my phone can fail,
Yet still I laugh, I'll find the trail.
Every wrong turn, a new surprise,
As I emerge with coffee eyes.

Threads of Intention

A thread unravels from my seam,
Ah well, it's all part of the scheme.
A thousand plans slip through my hands,
While I dream big of rockstar bands.

A note stuck to the fridge in pride,
Reminds me to enjoy the ride.
From mishaps bright, my heart will glow,
In this fabric of the go-with-the-flow.

Capturing Fleeting Moments

In the morning rush, I spilled my tea,
Got a laugh from the cat, as he stared at me.
Pants on backwards, what a sight to see,
Yet here I am, dancing with glee.

The clock ticks fast, as I forget my keys,
Waving to neighbors like they're old trees.
Trip on the sidewalk, oh such a tease,
But laughter erupts, and we aim to please.

The Pendulum of Choice

Should I wear the blue, or the bright red tie?
Both scream 'fancy' while I just sigh.
Maybe I'll flip a coin, oh my!
But it lands on the dog—guess I'll just fly.

Taco or curry? Decisions galore!
End up with leftovers; now that's a bore.
But stir-fried chaos brings laughter to the floor,
As the fridge sings a tune, who could ask for more?

Among the Stars of Fate

They say I'm a star, but I'm more like a dot,
One tiny speck in this cosmic plot.
Wishing on wishes, but take a shot—
My dreams were just pizza, now I'm tied in a knot.

I ponder my future, as I float on a cloud,
With broccoli stardust, feeling quite proud.
But the universe chuckles, under its shroud,
Turns out my destiny's just pizza, way loud!

The Mosaic of Events

Each event a piece, in a jigsaw game,
Some fit quite well, others feel lame.
Lost my shoe, but hey, who's to blame?
Jazz hands ensue, I dance without shame.

A slip and a slide, down the grocery aisle,
Mayonnaise tango, it's truly my style.
With a wink and a grin, I traverse each mile,
In this mad mosaic, I'm winning with guile.

The Craft of Meandering

In a world that spins like a top,
I wandered, hoping to stop.
With each turn, I lost my shoes,
Claimed by the dance of whims and blues.

My map has coffee stains and crumbs,
It's a treasure hunt for pats and hums.
I greet the squirrels with a bow,
They seem to know more than I allow.

Laughing at each twist I've met,
Falling down, but never upset.
Life's a tango with a twist,
A merry jig that can't be missed.

So here I sway, just passing through,
With no destination in view.
And as I roam, blissfully free,
Each silly step is all I need to see.

Fables of Chance

The dice were tossed, oh what a sight,
I rolled a six, then lost the fight!
The fortune teller laughed at my fate,
Turns out she just ate too much plate.

I found a penny, picked it up,
Then spilled my drink in a hiccup.
Lemonade wishes, a side of fries,
In this game of luck, no one can be wise.

Counting stars, I dropped my snack,
Wishing on crumbs, I can't take back.
The moon winked at my silly hue,
And then I danced, just to break through.

In this circus of fate and glee,
I grab the popcorn, let it be.
Every twist, a comedic scene,
As if I'm living someone else's dream.

The Divine Equation

With numbers swirling in my mind,
I've lost the sum of every kind.
I tried to solve for X and Y,
But all I got was a soggy pie.

God must be laughing at the mess,
Equating my stress to a fancy dress.
With every problem that I meet,
I find the answer in a big old seat.

Creating formulas of zigzag fun,
With silly outcomes, never done.
The square root of joy is always high,
While the multiplication of hope won't die.

Adding laughter, subtracting frowns,
Around and around, the merry-go-rounds.
In this math of oddities and jests,
We find the humor in our quests.

Dreams Dressed in Possibility

Wrapped in fabric of what could be,
My dreams parade, all wild and free.
I tried to stitch them back to place,
But they insisted on a silly race.

With colors bright, my visions twirl,
A ribbon dancer in a spunky whirl.
Each thread a laugh, each button a cheer,
Who knew whims could bring such gear?

Sailing boats made of bubblegum,
Drifting through clouds, what a fun sum!
The skies toss dreams like confetti bold,
And I catch them all, not letting go.

So here's to the fabric of our schemes,
Dressed as jesters, full of dreams.
In this quirky show, we take the chance,
To dance in all our silly pants.

The Dance of the Unforeseen

Twirl and stumble, what a sight,
A misstep here, but what delight!
The shoes may squeak, the rhythm's off,
Yet laughter echoes, who wouldn't scoff?

Around we whirl in pure surprise,
With wiggles, giggles, and bulging eyes.
The tune may falter, the beat may pause,
But we dance on without a cause!

Forgotten steps, but that's okay,
We laugh the awkwardness away.
In every spin, a fumble shines,
Embracing chaos, the world's designs.

So grab a partner, don't think twice,
Embrace the tumble, roll the dice.
For in this dance, we find the thrill,
A joyful chaos that fits the bill!

Patterns in the Chaos

In the mess of socks, a hidden art,
Missing shoes play a crucial part.
Life draws lines in mismatched hues,
Finding patterns in the blues.

Tangled cords and crumpled dreams,
Plot twists pop up like wild streams.
What's the plan? Who needs a clue?
When chaos sings, we laugh anew.

The cereal spills, the milk goes splat,
A masterpiece inside a spat!
We try to tidy, but it's in vain,
The joy of mess is worth the gain.

So let's embrace this lovely mess,
In structured chaos, we'll find success.
A jumbled palette, a colorful spread,
With laughter and joy, we'll break the bed!

The Scripted Chaos

A plot it seems, but who can tell?
With twists and turns that go so well.
The hero trips, the villain eats,
And laughter bursts from all the seats.

One more take, and still we fumble,
The script is bent; we gleefully stumble.
What's the next line? No need to fret,
In this fine play, there's no regret.

The director yells; we pause with fright,
Then break into giggles, what a sight!
Improvised quips, a kooky blend,
In every line, let laughter bend.

So here we are, a motley crew,
With scripted chaos that feels brand new.
Put on your hat, let's break the mold,
In this wild play, be brave and bold!

Journeys Without Maps

Off we go, towards who knows where,
With snacks in hand and a dash of flair.
The road, it twists, and so do we,
Finding joys where the wild winds flee.

A wrong turn here, a laugh out loud,
Met a cow that seemed quite proud.
Maps are for those who like to plan,
We roam free, where the whimsy spans.

Got lost in fields of daisies bright,
Found treasure in a firefly light.
With every mishap, our spirits soared,
On this wild journey, we're never bored.

So here's to paths that lead us astray,
The fun of wandering, come what may.
With giggles galore and hearts so light,
Each journey shared is pure delight!

The Hidden Design

In a world where ducks wear hats,
And cats speak in rhymes so flat,
I trip over thoughts like tangled yarn,
Wondering why I skipped the barn.

Every misstep leads me to cheer,
A dance with a lamp post, my dear,
With each twist I find unexpected joy,
Like a kid with a giant toy.

The maps we draw are fun to see,
Yet often lead to a mystery,
As squirrels laugh at our grand plans,
With acorns thrown by little hands.

So here I stand, a jumbled mess,
Yet smiling wide, I must confess,
For in chaos there's a hidden grace,
Like ice cream falling on my face.

Embracing the Unknown

In the dark where shadows play,
I dance with fears that lead astray,
But when I twirl, I find surprise,
The moon winks back, no need for ties.

A cereal box forms my guide,
With cartoon maps where monsters hide,
I take a leap without a net,
And stumble on the secrets I beget.

What if the path leads to a stew?
With flavors strange, maybe just a shoe,
I'll taste each moment, bite by bite,
And laugh at every quirky sight.

So here's my toast to what's not clear,
I'll sip my drink and raise a cheer,
For in the odd, I may unearth,
The joy that comes from crazy mirth.

Signs Written in Stars

I gazed upon the twinkling night,
Searching for hints in the starlight bright,
But found a goat, wearing shades of blue,
And it winked at me, who knew it too?

The constellations dance and tease,
Like giant puppets caught in a breeze,
With arrows pointing everywhere,
To pizza shops with gourmet fare.

My horoscope said it's time to play,
To jump around in a silly ballet,
So I joined a crowd of crazed balloon,
Who floated by singing a goofy tune.

Each star a guide, or so I think,
But they merely laugh as I try to blink,
For in their sparkle lies no straight road,
Just a confetti trail, an absurd ode.

The Road Less Traveled

Two paths diverged; I chose the mess,
With rubber ducks in my backpack, no less,
I skipped the crowd on a paper float,
Sailing through puddles in a coat.

A sign said 'Danger,' but what a bore,
I heard laughter and went for more,
With frogs in tuxedos leading the way,
I danced through the night, what a display!

Each twist and turn brought giggles anew,
With roadblocks of cake and bacon chew,
My GPS lost with glee in its tone,
Sent me to places I'd gladly own.

So here's to the road that goes off grid,
Where trees tell stories and no one hid,
For in the wacky mess of this ride,
I find that joy won't ever hide.

The Art of Letting Go

I tried to hold on tight, you see,
But my coffee said, "Just let it be!"
The socks disappeared, oh where'd they run?
Turns out they're off having some fun.

I waved goodbye to my old car keys,
They left a note saying, "Do as you please!"
The remote's a magician, poof, it's gone!
It must be playing tricks from dusk till dawn.

With every spill and every fall,
I learn to giggle, not take it all.
So here's the secret, you've got to know:
To truly embrace it, just let it flow.

In the end, it's a wacky ride,
With unexpected turns, and joy not to hide.
Letting go can tickle like a feather,
In this circus of life, we're all in together.

Embracing the Unexpected

I planned my day down to the minute,
But then the cat knocked over my limit!
Dinner was fish, but it turned to stew,
Thanks to the dog, who loves to chew.

The clock ticked fast, I lost track of time,
While searching for my snack, lost in a rhyme.
The rain said, "Surprise! No sun today!"
I danced in the puddles, come what may.

When in doubt, just roll with the flow,
Maybe try dancing, or a hat from Halo.
Unexpected joys are like hidden gold,
Each twist and turn, a story told.

Blame it on luck, or chance, or fate,
But isn't it fun when you're feeling great?
With smiles and laughter, onward we go,
Embracing the chaos, stealing the show!

A Kaleidoscope of Dreams

I dream of pizza flying in the sky,
With pepperoni clouds just floating by.
A rainbow of ice cream, what a delight,
Tastes like magic, in every bite.

Hats that sing and shoes that dance,
Imagine if socks could take a chance!
A world where unicorns paint the skies,
With sparkly wishes in baby blue ties.

Riding a turtle, slow and grand,
In a land where jellybeans grow in the sand.
Chasing the sunset, catching a breeze,
In a land of dreams where we do as we please.

So let's flip the pages, let's not be shy,
Life's a wacky ride, oh me, oh my!
With every twist, a bright serenade,
In this kaleidoscope, we've got it made!

The Compass Within

With a compass that spins, pointing who knows,
I'm lost in the woods with a trail of prose.
My heart sings loudly, though my map's askew,
Every step I take, it's a dance for two.

The stars are my guides on this wild trek,
With laughter echoing like a ship's old deck.
When life throws lemons, I juggle with flair,
Making lemonade from the icy air.

A squirrel high-fives me, what's up with that?
Every nook reveals treasures, like a jolly hat.
Whenever it's cloudy, I'll paint it bright,
With colors from dreams that twinkle at night.

So trust that compass, let it spin free,
In the heart of the whimsy, just be, simply be.
Because deep down inside, I've got the key,
To unlock the adventures that are waiting for me.

The Serenity of Flow

The river whispers tales untold,
As ducks glide by, so brave and bold.
A fish jumps high, it's quite a show,
While I sit here, just enjoying the flow.

Breezes tickle grass and trees,
A squirrel laughs, 'Hey, look at me!'
With every twist and turn I see,
The world's a joke, and I'm the key.

Sunshine dances, shadows play,
Who needs a map on a sunny day?
I follow whims, let worries go,
In this flowing stream, I'm happy to tow.

So raise a glass to chance and rhyme,
For we all know, it's a merry climb.
A moment's laugh, a silly span,
Just go with it, embrace the plan!

Seasons of Uncertainty

Winter brings snow and folks in coats,
While summer's all about the boats.
Spring is sneezing with pollen flare,
And fall? Well, it's just hard to care!

I'll wear my shorts when it's twenty below,
And celebrate warmth with a frosty glow.
Seasons change like a toddler's mood,
Each brings its charm, or just some food.

Count weekends like time's on sale,
Yet Monday wanders in, pale and frail.
Watch the clock, or just let it slide,
In the season of chaos, we might just hide.

So bring on the sun, or snow, or rain,
In this comedy, there's no real gain.
With every twist, the punchline's clear,
Embrace the wackiness, and hold it near!

The Canvas of Tomorrow

Today's a canvas, smeared with glee,
With splashes of mishaps, just wait and see.
Tomorrow waits, brushes in hand,
What colors it brings? It's all quite unplanned!

A splash of purple where green should be,
A dotted sky calls forth the sea.
With every stroke, uncertainty reigns,
But the laughter echoes, despite the stains.

Painting dreams with a clumsy brush,
Hoping for gold but landing on mush.
Yet each line tells tales, winks and grins,
In this gallery, we all fit in!

So dip the brush, make a delightful mess,
Who cares if it's chaos? It's happiness!
Tomorrow's tapestry, wild and bright,
Let's paint it together, with all our might!

Unfolding Futures

Tomorrow's map? Just a doodle and scribble,
With pathways that twist like a playful dribble.
We chase the sunrise, or maybe the moon,
Each step's an adventure, a whimsical tune.

What ifs and maybes dance in the air,
Like mismatched socks or creative hair.
With every turn, we grin and surprise,
For each unfolding brings new highs.

A fortune cookie? That's just dessert,
Promises scratchy, like a new-age shirt.
Navigating futures with laughter, not fear,
Let's toast to the chaos that brought us here!

So map it out, but don't be too rash,
With each curve and twist, we'll make quite the splash.
Life's a party, so let's join the fun,
For who knows the future? Just wait and run!

The Unraveled Map

I bought a map to find my way,
But it led me to a cabaret.
Dancing clowns and pie fights abound,
I lost the road that I had found.

With every turn, a silly sign,
"Here lies the spot for giant swine."
A compass, too, I thought was wise,
But it pointed me to donut pies.

My friends just laughed; they rolled their eyes,
As I claimed the map to be a prize.
In every twist, I found a joke,
At least I won a slice of cake.

So I embrace this tangled fate,
With giggles shared and laughter great.
The path may wind, but oh, what fun!
For every trip, there's a new pun.

When Stars Align

They say when stars align just right,
Great things will happen, take to flight.
But mine just winked and made a mess,
   Globes spinning fast, I must confess.

I tried to check my horoscope,
In hopes to find a bit of hope.
"Your day's a five; go eat some cheese,"
I laughed so hard, I dropped my keys.

The universe, it seems, likes games,
With cosmic jokes and wild refrains.
A streak of luck, a tumble here,
I tripped on stars while sipping beer.

In chaos, I can dance and twirl,
Finding joy in each crazy swirl.
So here's to fate—whatever's stored,
I'll take the laughs and not the bored.

In the Hands of Fortune

Fortune's dice are always thrown,
And I'm just here, all on my own.
I ventured forth with head held high,
And tripped on luck—oh me, oh my!

A scratch-off ticket made me grin,
"Win a million? Start with a pin!"
I scratched and scratched until I bled,
Turns out it wasn't gold, but lead.

I asked for fortune, just a taste,
But chaos danced with comic haste.
A slip, a trip, a pie in the face,
Oh, fortune, you're quite the case!

But in this game of twist and turn,
I've sopped up messes, felt the burn.
In laughter's arms, I wave goodbye,
To perfect plans that never fly.

A Dance with Uncertainty

I stepped onto the dance floor bright,
Where moves are random, pure delight.
With two left feet, I danced away,
My partner giggled, "That's okay!"

The music swirled, I lost my place,
But who needs rhythm in this space?
We spun and twirled, a tangled feat,
Our laughter made it all repeat.

I tried a dip, but missed the catch,
We both went down—a perfect match!
In every slip and twisted spin,
I found my joy, let chaos win.

So here's to dances without a cue,
Where every step is something new.
With silly grins and clumsy cheer,
Uncertainty's my partner here.

The Secret Dance of Moments

In a kitchen, a spoon takes a twirl,
Pasta's boiling, oh what a whirl.
Dance like no one's seeing, take a chance,
The cat looks on, judging the dance.

Jellybeans jump from the cupboard high,
Missed the target, oh my, oh my!
Laughter echoes, a silly ballet,
Whisking away the worries of the day.

A fridge that hums a silly tune,
Items inside, a wild cartoon.
The salad spins, it's gone quite mad,
Who knew moments could be so rad?

So grab your apron, join the spree,
Life's a joke, so giggle with glee.
In every second, find a frolic,
This dance of moments, rather iconic.

The Path of the Wandering Star

A star wandered off in the night,
Said, "Why not? I'll give it a flight!"
Got lost in a cloud, so fluffy and bright,
Fell into a joke with a disco light.

"Hey Moon, got any plans for the day?"
"I'm just here, hanging out, hey, hey!"
Together they giggled, shared a few crumbs,
Even stars know how to have fun, just hums.

In the cosmos, there's laughter and glee,
A galaxy party, just wait and see.
They twirl and they spin, like kids in the sand,
Conspiring to make the universe grand.

So if you're ever feeling quite far,
Just gaze at the sky, find your own star.
Wander like them, take a quirky route,
For in their dances, joy's never in doubt.

Unwritten Destinies

A blank page waits, oh what a tease,
With secret scribbles, if you please.
What if tomorrow tastes like pie?
Or maybe it's a dance party, oh my!

The future's a riddle, tangled and fun,
Like a cat on a counter, just on the run.
What's next for us? Who even knows?
Perhaps all we need are some garden hoses!

We flip a coin, heads or tails,
Its magic spins like fanciful tales.
Imagining worlds, so silly and grand,
Who wrote this story? Not quite as planned.

So laugh at the blankness, color it bright,
With crayons or giggles, bring it to light.
Unwritten pages, a canvas for glee,
In the book of adventures, be wild and free!

The Art of Transitions

From morning to night, what a bizarre trip,
Coffee in hand, balancing a sip.
Sweeping the floors, oh what a mess,
With socks on the dog—now that's success!

The clock ticks slowly, time takes a stroll,
Making toast while I search for my soul.
What's for dinner? A puzzle of dreams,
Yesterday's leftovers, or so it seems.

When seasons change, we shuffle and sway,
Jumping from summer straight into May.
Wearing mittens with sandals? Why not!
Life's unpredictable, like a spontaneous plot.

So here's to the shifts, the joyous and wild,
Embrace each moment, like a playful child.
Dance through the chaos, don't fret or resist,
In the art of transitions, there's humor, not mist.

Shadows of Fate

In a game of dice, we all roll,
Shadows nudge fate, oh, what a stroll!
Waking up late, as the sun takes a peek,
Do the socks match? Just call it unique.

Coffee spills like a wild dance,
Life's too short; let's take a chance!
The cat runs away with the mailman's hat,
A fitting crown for a royal sprawl!

Why is it framed like a jigsaw puzzle?
More pieces missing, oh what a tussle!
With laughter echoing in twilight's embrace,
The shadows twist into a silly race.

So raise your glass, here's to the plan,
To the unexpected, life's funny jam!
We trip and we fall, but what a delight,
In this circus of chaos, we find our light.

Navigating the Currents

Float on the river, where ducks wear crowns,
Paddles are wands in these silly towns.
Catch the breeze with a grin so wide,
Who knew a sandwich would be our guide?

The currents swirl, and the map's upside down,
A treasure chest filled with gummy bears, no frown!
Navigators giggle with each awkward turn,
Each twist of the fate, just more to learn.

Life's a boat ride in a kiddie pool,
Skipping along, acting like a fool.
The laughter bubbles, like soda pop fizz,
Sailing on dreams, what a funny whizz!

So put on your goggles, let's dive right in,
With joy as our compass, we're bound to win!
With wobbly adventures and friends by our side,
We laugh at the waves, on this wild ride.

The Fabric of Riddles

Threads of the day weave a quilt of cheer,
Every stitch whispers, "Oh let's not fear!"
Buttons of laughter, patterns so wild,
Tangled and twisted, just like a child.

The riddle of socks: where do they go?
In a world where missing socks steal the show!
Fabric of secrets, sewn tight with glee,
Who can decipher this tangled decree?

Spools of mischief, unraveled tales,
The dog wears a sweater, as truce prevails.
With spins and twirls, the colors collide,
Life's funny fabric can't be denied.

So let's knit together with laughter and song,
In this merry tapestry, we all belong!
Each riddle unraveled brings smiles anew,
With yarn in our hands, let's make something true.

Beyond the Veil of Time

Tick-tock goes the clock; who set it right?
Time wears a mustache; what a funny sight!
With a wave of the wand, now seconds rewind,
A giggle escapes, as we dance unconfined.

The past is a jester, with tricks up its sleeve,
Making us ponder what we believe.
Fossils of moments trapped in a jar,
Can laughter really echo from far?

Stumbling through timelines, all out of whack,
Lost in a maze, but who needs a map?
With each tick we twist, new jokes we create,
The punchline hits hard, and oh, isn't it great?

So let's pull back the curtains, give time a cheer,
For the struggles and giggles, let's keep them near!
In this whimsical dance, we'll twirl and spin,
Beyond the veil, where adventures begin!

Ripples of Chance

A penny dropped, what will it bring?
A wild dance of fate doing its thing.
You trip on a stone, then meet a friend,
Is it chaos or magic? Let's pretend!

Cats chase shadows, dogs chase their tails,
We make plans just to see how it fails.
With every misstep, a new chance to laugh,
Sailing our boats on a lopsided path.

So sprinkle some joy in uneasy waters,
Blame it on fortune, or sleep like otters.
Who knows what's next? A pie in the sky?
Or maybe a dance with an octopus, why?

Now raise your glass to the quirky and bold,
For the stories we gather make us feel old.
Each rippling moment, a giggle in time,
We're all just a part of this absurd rhyme.

Echoes of What Could Be

In a coffee shop, plans tumble and sway,
Promises made on a whim, come what may.
A napkin scribbled with dreams oh-so-bright,
Ends up as laughter at the end of the night.

Oh, the could haves parade with a sigh,
Like socks mismatched, we give them a try.
A job that went south, just left us confused,
But oh, could it be more fun being amused?

In the end, we smile at our messy designs,
Roller coasters built with crooked lines.
With echoes that bounce like a kid on the floor,
We laugh and we stumble, then ask for more!

So let's toast to the battles we didn't quite win,
With winks at the things that may never begin.
The fiddles and flukes that keep us awake,
In the echoes of dreams, there's always a shake.

Beyond the Horizon

A kite takes flight, meandering high,
Wishes blow forward, like clouds in the sky.
We follow the colors, a curious bunch,
With every gust, it's lunch on a crunch!

Beyond the horizon, where oddities dwell,
Are unicorns dancing with a cat named Mel.
Silly adventures we hope to embrace,
With hiccups of joy, in this zany race.

Each twist and turn, a fresh slice of cake,
A mondo of choices, let's bravely partake.
With maps that are drawn in crayon and cheer,
We'll conquer the worlds we've imagined right here!

So let's march on forward, and cheerfully sing,
Grab your umbrella, for who knows what the wind will bring?
In our whimsical journey, let's laugh without fear,
For beyond every horizon, the fun is so near.

A Symphony of Serendipity

A tune starts playing, oh what a surprise,
Notes leap and prance right before our eyes.
Every off-key moment brings us a grin,
In the symphony of chaos, let's whirl and spin!

A bus that shows late and leads to a show,
With laughter and dance, we just go with the flow.
A mix-up in dinner, but hey, what's a meal?
A feast for the senses, that's part of the deal!

The music of mishaps, a whimsical beat,
Plays on as we twirl with two left feet.
What would we be without blunders that shine?
The symphony of serendipity divine!

So raise up your glasses, let irony thrive,
For in every hiccup, we feel so alive.
With laughter our anthem, joy as our creed,
In this playful orchestra, we all take the lead!

The Thread of Destiny

A tailor stitches moments tight,
With laughter woven in the night.
The fabric frays in unexpected leaps,
As we wear hats of dreams and heaps.

Each button pops like a secret joke,
Stitching smiles in every cloak.
Some threads are tangled, others fray,
Yet we dance through life, come what may.

With scissors in hand, we clip and fade,
Crafting a suit from the chaos made.
Every cut a funny tale to choose,
In this wardrobe, nothing to lose.

So, let's laugh at this patchy attire,
Each snag a giggle, each knot a fire.
For in this garment of playful jest,
We'd find our comfort and maybe the rest.

Serendipitous Journeys

The road is paved with silly chance,
With detours that invite a dance.
We stumble, trip, and then we slide,
On stray adventures, we take pride.

A wrong turn leads to ice cream bliss,
Who knew fate would give us this?
With every twist, we burst in glee,
Finding treasures unexpectedly.

The map is scribbled with crayon hopes,
As we navigate through goofy slopes.
And every sign offers a laugh,
Pointing us to the fun path's half.

So grab your gear, let's hit the road,
Routine is nice, but it gets old.
With every twist and turn we find,
Serendipity is quite the grind.

Forks in the Path

Here we stand at the crossroads wide,
One way is smooth, the other a ride.
With a wink, we shrug and flip a coin,
Life's twisty trails we shall purloin.

To the left, a sign says 'Boring' route,
To the right, 'Adventures no doubt.'
We throw caution, and purposeless maps,
For fun's the goal, not solemn japs.

With sandwiches packed, we venture bold,
Choosing the path less traveled, we're told.
Each fork a laugh, a cheeky jibe,
Unraveling giggles, our lovely tribe.

So let us wander where the wild things grow,
Turning dilemmas into a show.
For every choice we make along the way,
Is a punchline, I'd happily say.

The Puzzle of Existence

Life's not a puzzle with perfect fits,
It's jumbled pieces that cause the whits.
Some corners miss, some edges fray,
Yet we giggle as we play the game today.

With pieces upside down and askew,
We shove the wrong bits, hoping for glue.
A duck in the middle of a grand parade,
We laugh 'til we cry, a roadmap remade.

The picture's fuzzy, colors clash bright,
Yet smiles emerge from our silly plight.
Each piece tells a story, a whimsical spin,
Of mishaps, giggles, where we begin.

So here's to the puzzle, a fun little mess,
Embracing the chaos, we'll never stress.
For in this scramble of twisty designs,
Lies the beauty of folly, where laughter shines.

The Essence of Unraveled Threads

In the tapestry of silly dreams,
The threads often fray, or so it seems.
I tried to sew a patch of cheer,
But ended up lost, oh dear, oh dear!

The needle slipped and my plans went wild,
Stitching together the thoughts of a child.
I laugh at the mess, it's pure delight,
A quilt of chaos that feels just right.

With every knot, a lesson learned,
Each twist and turn, my stomach churned.
But with each laugh, I find my way,
In this wacky game we call today.

So here's to the fabric, frayed and torn,
A patchwork of moments where joy is born.
Let's dance in the threads that bind us tight,
In this joyful mess, everything feels bright.

Portrait of a Wandering Heart

My heart's a traveler, never at rest,
On a quest for snacks, it's on a quest!
It wanders through fields, and skips over stones,
Chasing after laughter, it never moans.

It stops for a moment to sniff at the flowers,
Then rushes ahead, forgetting the hours.
With a squirrelly grin and a bounce in its beat,
It makes friends with the grass, oh what a feat!

But then comes the time to take a small break,
To ponder the choices and mistakes that we make.
"Where have I been?" it asks with a grin,
"Wherever I go, let the fun now begin!"

So here's to the journeys that take us afar,
In search of a laugh, or a bright-shining star.
With a heart that wanders, let's boldly depart,
On this silly adventure, we make our own art.

The Spiral of Experiences

Round and round in a dizzying whirl,
Life's a dance, give it a twirl.
Each step is a giggle, a chuckle or two,
In this spiral of joy, there's always something new.

I tried to keep up with the pace of the ride,
But tripped on my shoelace and slid to the side.
The laughter erupted, everyone cheered,
"More spins and tumbles!" they joyously steered.

From moments of wonder to stumbles and falls,
The spiral keeps turning, oh how it enthralls!
With a wink and a grin, we embrace the unknown,
For in every mishap, a new joy is sown.

So let's twirl together in this merry-go-round,
Where laughter is plenty, and joy can be found.
We'll create memories, let's dance and take flight,
In this spiral of joy, everything feels right.

Through the Looking Glass

Peering through glass, I see my reflection,
A quirky facade of sheer imperfection.
The smile gets wobbly, the eyebrows won't stay,
It's hard to be serious in such a funny way.

What is this world beyond this thin wall?
A circus of laughter, a vibrant free-for-all!
With costumes and jokes, and pies in the sky,
I reach for the handle, oh my, oh my!

In stepping outside, I tumble with glee,
A kaleidoscope spin of absurdity.
The shadows are silly, the colors delight,
In this topsy-turvy world, everything's bright.

So let's flip the coin, take a chance on a dare,
For in this grand mirror, there's magic to share.
With humor our compass, let's find where we fit,
Through the looking glass, let's revel in it!

Seeds of Tomorrow in Today's Soil

In gardens where wild thoughts do grow,
We plant our hopes, just to see them blow.
Water with giggles, sunshine with glee,
Wait for the bloom, or a squirrel's grand spree.

We dig for answers, but find only worms,
Expecting big harvests from tiny little firms.
A sprout of a dream, might just go astray,
But oh, what a show if it dances away!

With shovels of laughter and buckets of fun,
Each misstep brings joy, like a bright summer sun.
So let's toss some seeds, see what they might be,
Maybe carrots, or laughter, or a dancing bee!

When aiming for greatness, don't take it too hard,
For weeds have their stories, each a quirky bard.
So here's to the plots where our worries won't toll,
In the gardens of goof, we shall find our whole!

A Journey Through the Labyrinth of Now

In the maze of the moment, we skip and we twirl,
Winding through options like a paper unfurl.
Each corner a chuckle, a twist and a turn,
Forget what we seek; it's the fun we will earn.

The signs say 'detour' yet we forge ahead,
Chuckling at life like it's made out of bread.
With breadcrumbs of laughter, we light up the dark,
Chasing the echoes, we find quite the spark.

Every pathway we take is a laugh or a chance,
Who knew all these choices could lead to a dance?
Round and round we roam, with nary a clue,
But isn't it grand? Here's a cheer, just for you!

We'll wander forever and never grow wise,
For in being a fool, the best treasure lies.
So here's to our journey, no matter the maze,
Embracing the silly, we'll bask in the blaze!

The Compass of Reassurance in Dilemmas

With a compass that wiggles, and points to the sky,
We question our choices, and wonder why.
Every wrong turn feels like a thrill,
Every 'oops' moment, gives life a grand fill.

A map made of giggles, directions unclear,
Navigating mishaps, with never a fear.
For when we get lost, we just laugh out aloud,
The right path unravels, and we're quite the crowd!

In the depths of confusion, we find a great beat,
As we salsa through chaos, with some shuffling feet.
Each dilemma a puzzle, unique and absurd,
With laughter as fuel, our worries deterred.

Shining through mishaps, like stars in the night,
Our compass of chuckles leads us to light.
So fear not the bumps; they're just part of the dance,
For in the wild waltz, we take every chance!

Serene Acceptance in the Midst of Waves

On shores where the laughter meets bubbles and foam,
We jump with the tides, not feeling alone.
Each splash is a chuckle, each wave a surprise,
As we float on our worries, we rise with the skies.

Embracing the ripples, we twirl with the swell,
For who needs a plan when chaos can tell?
With a surfing board made of joy, we ride on,
Tumbling through troubles until they are gone.

Each wave is a jest, as it tickles our toes,
And losing our balance, well that's how it goes!
With smiles like suns, we dance in the spray,
Finding peace in the jest, oh what a grand play!

So let's surf through the storms, with a wink and a cheer,
Embracing the foibles, let laughter steer clear.
In the sea of acceptance, let joy lead the way,
For amidst all the waves, it's a marvelous play!

The Palette of Decisions

With colors bright, I paint my fate,
A splash of red, then I contemplate.
I mix in blue, what a sight,
Oh dear, is that a shade of fright?

Brush in hand, I start to blend,
A swirl of choice, where does it end?
Do I need orange, or is it pink?
Wait, what was I doing? Let me think!

The canvas laughs at my confused face,
Each choice I make seems out of place.
But in the chaos, joy appears,
Who knew my mess could spark such cheers?

In this art of doing, not just planning,
I find the fun, and it's quite outstanding.
So here I scribble, wild and free,
With pots of paint, I'll just let it be!

Navigating Through the Storm

On a boat made of dreams, I set my sail,
The skies grow dark, but I won't pale.
Waves dance high, I grip the wheel,
Is that lightning, or just my meal?

Paddling hard, I'm losing grace,
Why did I think I'd win this race?
I shout to clouds, 'Do lend a hand!'
They rumble back, 'You're in command!'

The compass spins—it's gone awry,
Should I steer left or simply cry?
With every gust, I laugh and say,
Who needs a map? Let's drift away!

In this tempest, I find my groove,
Sailing madly while I move.
A pirate's heart in a storm anew,
What's better than chaos, just me and you!

The Voyage of Uncertainty

With a suitcase packed, I board the train,
Where it goes, I'm not certain, just riding the vein.
I check my ticket, oh what a blunder,
Turns out it's just a trip to the under!

The conductor laughs, he's seen it all,
A traveler lost is often their call.
"Just grab a snack; you'll be just fine,"
I smile at the chaos, is it truly divine?

Each station flies by, like a quest,
I wave at the people—it's quite the fest!
A journey uncertain, yet filled with cheer,
It's the mishaps that count, my dear?

With every whistle, I toast to the ride,
Embracing the wild, I'll never hide.
So here's to the unknown, I raise a cheer,
Onward I wander—adventure is near!

Whispers Among the Pages

In a library tucked away from the sun,
Pages giggle, oh what fun!
Each story a riddle, a twist, a dance,
Who knew a book could hold such romance?

I flip through the chapters, my heart in a race,
One villain's plot creates quite the space.
I pause, I chuckle at the tale's turn,
In this world of words, I yearn and learn.

A character fumbles, a plot thickens fast,
Who wrote this mess? Can it ever last?
Yet in each blunder, wisdom takes flight,
Page after page, I find sheer delight.

So here, among whispers, I dare to stay,
In the chaos of stories, I'll laugh all day.
For in every novel, be it sad or bright,
I discover the joy that's tucked out of sight.

The Serendipity of Missteps

I tripped over my own two feet,
While trying to look so neat.
The flowers laughed, the birds cheer,
'Falling's just a part of cheer!'

I spilled my drink upon the floor,
Thought I'd failed, but then I swore.
A slip, a slide—what's this I see?
A party formed, just thanks to me!

With every twist and turn I make,
I find new paths with every ache.
In jumbled steps, the fun resides,
So here's to those quirky rides!

Embrace the chaos, dance the dance,
Every blunder teaches chance.
So laugh along, don't take the shot,
In every fumble, joy is caught!

Chance Encounters Under Starry Skies

I met a cat while counting stars,
He claimed he'd traveled near and far.
With each purr, he'd share a tale,
Of fishy friends and moonlit sail.

A dog jumped in, quite out of breath,
Said, 'Life's a chase, 'til one of us' death!'
We all laughed in the midnight air,
Under the moon, without a care.

A raccoon joined, with a shiny prize,
Turns out, it's just old fries!
Under twinkling lights we found,
A treasure trove of stories sound.

In random meets, the magic shines,
Where whimsy laughs and fate intertwines.
So throw your plans into the night,
For chance encounters can be a delight!

Dreams Cast upon Shifting Sands

I built a castle made of dreams,
But tides came in, or so it seems.
With each wave, my plans washed out,
Yet laughter swirled in playful shout.

I dreamed of gold, a shining moon,
But then my shovel found a spoon!
I pondered hard, a wise old crab,
'Dig a new path, create a fab!'

The sands beneath can twist and turn,
But fleeting moments help us learn.
With every grain that slips away,
New dreams take shape in their own way.

So gather 'round, let's play the game,
And sing our whims without a shame.
In shifting sands, we live and glide,
For joy resides where dreams collide!

Embracing the Chaos in Silence

In quiet corners, chaos stirs,
While silence brews with quiet purrs.
The dishes dance without a care,
And spoons take flight through icy air.

A not-so-friendly sock may hide,
But treasures wait where messes bide.
Beneath the heap, a smile shines through,
In every mess, something new to view.

So sail the seas of cluttered dreams,
Where laughter bursts at the seams.
In silent chaos, find your glee,
The heart of fun is wild and free!

So raise a toast to the disarray,
For even chaos has its play.
In every chuckle, every sigh,
We dance through chaos, you and I!

Whispers of a Forgotten Blueprint

In a world drawn without a map,
Funny things happen, oh, it's a trap.
The architect sneezed while designing,
Now we're all just winging, no hiding.

Each twist and turn feels like a jest,
Maybe it's fate wearing a vest.
Coffee spills, a laugh, then we go,
What's the plan? We just don't know.

We dance on floors with missing tiles,
Laugh at rabbits wearing big smiles.
The blueprint's lost, but that's okay,
We'll find our joy in silly play.

So grab your hat, let's take a spin,
Who knows where this ride will begin?
Maybe we're stars in this grand design,
Cheers to the chaos, it's all quite fine!

The Jigsaw Puzzle of Existence

A piece from the cat, a corner misplaced,
Is this life's game or just something chased?
Trying to fit in, it's quite absurd,
Yet here we laugh, flying like a bird.

Edges all tangled, colors don't match,
Searching for joy, oh, what a catch!
The picture is fuzzy, it doesn't quite blend,
Yet every mishap turns into a friend.

We're flipping pieces, finding our way,
Cracking up at the mess every day.
Some days it's fun, some days it's a bore,
But oh, the stories, who could ask for more?

So let's embrace this chaotic phase,
With puzzle pieces lost in a daze.
Together we'll chuckle; it's part of the dance,
In this jigsaw game, we'll take a chance!

Threads of Fate in a Woven Tapestry

A tapestry tangled, colors collide,
Threading through chaos, we glide and slide.
Each knot tells a story, some tangled, some neat,
Life's little mishaps, oh, what a feat.

The needle slips, and oops, what a fold,
Is this a design or just something bold?
Woven with laughter, the fabric flows free,
A quilt of nonsense, as cozy as can be.

There are threads of fortune, and threads of woe,
But mix them together, and watch the show!
A patch here, a patch there, we sew it with cheer,
This whimsical weave, let's give a big cheer.

So grab your yarn, let's stitch on the go,
The tapestry's wild; it's starting to glow.
With every mistake, we're stitching with glee,
In this fabric of fate, we're forever free!

Navigating the Maze of Uncertainty

In a corn maze filled with strange signs,
Every wrong turn leads to great finds.
Dizzy from laughter, we stumble and trip,
Who knew lost directions could be such a trip?

Left or right, oh where do we go?
The paths intertwine like a stand-up show.
We giggle and squirm, then turn around,
Every dead end brings more joy to be found.

Dark corners whisper, "Try going straight!"
Is that a joke or a twist of fate?
But hey, let's embrace this thrilling adventure,
With laughter as fuel, we'll never lose our center.

So here's to the maze, with laughter and cheer,
Let's toast to the journey, there's nothing to fear.
In this tangled web of twists and more spins,
We find our way out, where the fun begins!

The Road Less Traveled by Design

I took a path with ducks and cows,
Thought I'd find wisdom, but all I found
Was a goat with a grin, and muddy brows,
He chewed my map, I laughed, confound!

Trees whispered secrets as I walked slow,
A squirrel gave a nod, quite debonair,
Yet, lost in thought, I missed the show,
A raccoon danced, without a care!

Potholes sang tunes like a bumpy ride,
My feet were tired, but the laughter soared,
In a world so wacky, I'll just abide,
Turns out the journey was the reward!

So here's a toast to the offbeat way,
With mud on my shoes and joy in my heart,
Every twist and turn makes a perfect sway,
What's planned isn't always the best part!

Mosaic of Moments in Time

Every tick of the clock makes a small splash,
Like a child with a pie, oh what a scene!
Some dreams are timid, some dreams are brash,
Creating a mosaic, a funny machine.

I spilled coffee on yesterday's plan,
Wiped it with laughter and crumbs from my toast,
Each moment a canvas, I'm quite the fan,
Of the chaos I cherish, it's what I love most.

A cat danced through a well-worn page,
As I scribbled thoughts in a reckless sprawl,
Embracing the mess, setting the stage,
Are those giggles? Oh, they answer my call!

In this gallery of silly youth,
Even missteps can shine like gold,
Navigating mishaps reveals the truth,
That joy is an art, and I'm bold!

Patterns Beneath the Surface of Delay

The clock tick-tocks with a cheeky grin,
As I wait for life to hand me the reins,
My plans on a ferris wheel, round and round,
Like juggling squirrels, it's all in my veins.

Traffic lights blink in a grand charade,
Dips and turns of fate's odd ballet,
Winging it wildly, I'm not dismayed,
For every snag is a comedic play!

Pending like clouds with a hint of a storm,
I find joy in the pauses, a splendid game,
Patterns emerge, so unexpected, so warm,
In lines that wander, I'm rarely the same.

So here's to the wait, the funny delay,
With twinkling eyes, I embrace the fun,
Each moment an adventure, come what may,
With laughter in tow, I'm well on the run!

The Symphony of Unforeseen Rhythms

Life's a tune where the notes go astray,
A kazoo joins in, oh, what a sound!
The drummer's confused yet keeps up the play,
And the audience chuckles, the joy is profound.

Dancing to beats that we never planned,
With a shoe on my head, I'm a sight to see,
In this silly concert, all lend a hand,
To harmonize chaos, how fancy, my glee!

Accidental solos burst out with pride,
When the trumpet's a plant from my friend's art,
But the laughter that's woven can never hide,
In a show of entangled, good-natured heart.

So let's strum our quirks, dance out of tune,
With brave serenades and odd little blows,
For the symphony's best when the rhythms balloon,
In the laughter-filled echoes, anything goes!

Tides of Time and the Flow of Choices

The clock ticks loud, a comical sound,
With choices that tumble and tumble around.
We ponder and fret, yet chuckle with glee,
At the mess we've made of our grand destiny.

Each wave that rolls, brings a twist and a turn,
We aim for the moon, but just crash and burn.
Yet through all the chaos, we stumble and sway,
Finding joy in the knots that we twist on our way.

The Unseen Hand Behind Our Steps

An unseen force pulls us here and there,
Like puppets in strings, without much care.
We dance on the stage, with a grin and a hop,
As plans tumble down, like a poorly made mop.

We trip on our shoelaces, blame the divine,
But laugh at the mess, 'cause it's all by design.
With a wink and a nudge, the cosmos will poke,
Reminding us all, that it's good to be broke.

Sketches of a Future Unfolding

With crayons in hand, we sketch out our fate,
But scribbles and doodles just make us relate.
Each stroke is a memory, a laugh or a sigh,
A masterpiece growing, as we just get by.

Though the colors may blur in a whimsical dance,
We wade through the muddle, embracing the chance.
For life's big canvas is splattered with glee,
And who knew the future would be such a spree?

Echoes of Yesterdays Yet to Come

In a loop of chuckles, we reminisce bright,
About blunders that seemed oh-so-wrong at first sight.
Yet echoes of laughter, they stack up like cheese,
A fondness for felonies that tickle with ease.

The past tries to wave, but the future's in play,
With pranks from tomorrow that's here for the day.
So let's toast to the fumbles that lead us to fun,
In the never-ending circus where all of us run.

The Glow of What May Be

In a world where cats rule the day,
And dogs just dance in dismay.
We chase the sun and trip on shoes,
While laughing at our silly blues.

A sandwich falls, and birds rejoice,
We eat our lunch; it's their choice.
With ever-changing whims of fate,
We toast a snack—let's celebrate!

Through sparkly lights and joyful cheer,
We weave our dreams, year after year.
With pizza slices flying high,
We share a wink and a pie in the sky.

So join the jest, let's laugh and spin,
For who knows where this trip has been?
With every twist, a tale unfolds,
In the glow of maybes, the future beholds.

Echoes of Surprise

A squirrel dances on my lawn,
As I sip coffee, yawning at dawn.
With a jug of milk and some sweet cake,
I ponder if I should just bake.

Why does the toaster always glitch?
Burnt bread serves as a little hitch.
Yet life pursues with comic flair,
Like socks lost in the washer's snare.

A spaghetti strand clings to my shoe,
And they say pasta's just good for two.
While I trip over my own two feet,
A circus act no one can beat!

In every stumble, laughter rings,
An ode to the joy that surprise brings.
For even when plans go off the rails,
It's the echoes of laughter that prevails.

Fluid Paths of Existence

I took a turn, ended in a ditch,
Why do GPS systems always glitch?
With fruit in hand, I found a pond,
While ducks quack till I feel quite conned.

Navigating this wiggly maze,
Each step ahead leads to silly crazes.
I slip on yogurt, the dogs all bark,
A splash of joy ignites a spark.

As time leads us down whacky lanes,
I find my heart in silly gains.
From fiery tacos to lumpy stew,
It's twists of fate that make me woo!

Hope floats on midnight's frothy tide,
Adventure springs from where voices collide.
Every unplanned turn's a delight,
Let's ride these paths into the night!

The Symmetry of Struggle

I woke today with a quest in mind,
To find the left sock I can't find.
As I scrape the fridge for a snack,
I wonder if I've lost my knack.

Bulging bags and a pan askew,
Cooking's tough when you're half-cooked too.
Lost in a world of culinary woe,
Yet giggles rise as I bravely go.

The cat walks by with that knowing stare,
It seems she senses I'm unaware.
Things can tumble, and chaos ensues,
But in the chaos, I find my muse.

With every twist, missteps abound,
In this grand circus we're all just clowns.
The symmetry is in how we cope,
Trading woes for bursts of hope.

When Shadows Dance with Light

In the evening glow, shadows play,
Chasing the sun, they twirl away.
A whisper of laughter, a giggle in the breeze,
Who knew darkness could move with such ease?

They flirt and prance, with no care in sight,
Shadow and light, what a quirky delight!
A tumble here, a skip over there,
Oh, life's little jokes are beyond all compare!

With beams of the sun tickling the ground,
Laughter erupts with each twist and round.
As shadows cackle, the day starts to fade,
Life's a grand circus, and we're all just played!

So let's twirl with shadows, let laughter be free,
When light takes a bow, join in the spree.
For in this grand show, we all have our part,
So dance with your shadows, it's the best kind of art!

Curves of Destiny in the Unknown

On roads that wind and twist ahead,
You might trip on dreams you thought were dead.
With each bend, a new surprise awaits,
Curves like candy canes, oh, what fun debates!

The GPS broke, but hey, that's okay,
Just follow the giggles and lead the way.
Who needs a map when you've got good cheer?
Curves of mishaps, in chaos I steer!

Navigating life like a wiggly worm,
Dancing in circles, a twirly long term.
A detour to laughter, a pit stop for pie,
Oh, these twists and turns make the sweetest high!

So grab your compass, let giggles align,
Each curve brings more fun—oh, isn't it fine?
In this adventure, just keep your heart light,
For unknown destinations can spark pure delight!

The Art of Expecting the Unexpected

I woke up this morning, the sun on my face,
But tripped on my shoelace and fell with such grace.
A toaster malfunction, toast flew across the room,
I laughed at the chaos, oh, what a boom!

With every new fumble, surprises abound,
Stumbling over life like it's a playground.
A pigeon stole my sandwich, how rude was that?
Finding humor in mishaps, oh, imagine that!

A knock at the door, it's the neighbor's cat,
This furry surprise simply won't chat.
I chuckle and wonder about today's design,
What lays around the corner, perhaps a punchline?

So welcome the oddities, embrace the bizarre,
For every twist leads to laughter, a sparkling star.
In the art of expectation, let spontaneity reign,
After all, humor is life's sweet champagne!

Fragmented Mirrors Reflecting Aspirations

In shards of glass, I see my dreams,
Like jigsaw puzzles in mismatched beams.
A glimpse of the future, a twinkle of hope,
Fragments of laughter, we learn how to cope.

With all this reflection, who needs a guide?
These broken mirrors make chaos our slide.
A snicker, a giggle, a wink in the glare,
What if we find joy hiding somewhere?

Every broken piece tells tales of a quest,
Showing us moments where fun is the best.
In the mosaic of mishaps, we paint our own way,
Finding humor in dreams that led us astray!

So here's to the mirrors, both cracked and whole,
Together they shape us, they make us feel whole.
In this playful patchwork, our futures align,
Embrace the absurd; oh, isn't it divine?

Shifting Sands of Tomorrow

In a world where we flip a coin,
The universe laughs, don't you join?
Plans like jelly on a warm plate,
Chance dances, oh, isn't it great?

We march to the beat of our own drum,
Stumbling through, feeling quite numb,
The future wiggles, it might mislead,
But isn't the chaos what we all need?

With every step, the ground may shift,
A comedy show, we're the main gift,
We're all just jesters, doing our dance,
In this big circus, we take our chance.

So hold your breath, and follow the twist,
Embrace the goofy, don't let it be missed,
Tomorrow awaits, like a fun surprise,
In shifting sands, our laughter will rise.

Echoes of a Whimsical Journey

Pack up your bags, it's time for a trip,
With socks on our hands, we let it rip,
The map is a doodle, the roads are a guess,
As we dance with the ducks, our lives are a mess.

Chasing rainbows that lead to the sky,
With hiccups and giggles, oh my, oh my,
We sail on a teacup, flying so high,
Each stumble a punchline, as time passes by.

A journey of whimsy, where snacks are our gold,
And the stories we gather, they never get old,
With a wink and a nod, we leap through the day,
In echoes of laughter, we lose our way.

So let's toast to the strangeness, the quirks that we find,
In this jolly parade, leave your worries behind,
For in every mishap, joy has its space,
Together we wander, at our own silly pace.

The Intricate Weave

With threads of confusion, we knit our own fate,
Stitching together, it's never too late,
Buttons of laughter, pockets of cheer,
A patchwork of moments, stitched with good beer.

Patterns emerge in the wildest of twists,
As we fumble and tumble, our dreams on a list,
Frogs playing chess near the edge of a brook,
In this tapestry strange, take a curious look.

Every loop tells a story, each knot holds a grin,
In this wacky creation, we all play to win,
So what if it's messy, we wear it with pride,
In the intricate weave, there's no place to hide.

So gather your stitches, and throw in a jibe,
With each playful fold, in this crazy vibe,
We're all just creators, using what's near,
In a world made of yarn, let's spread the good cheer.

Symphony of the Unscripted

With a trumpet that squeaks and a kazoo in tow,
We compose a grand tune with no need to show,
Each note is a giggle, each rest is a sigh,
In this symphony wild, we just dance and fly.

The conductor's a cat, with a flick of its tail,
Leading us onward in this whimsical tale,
From polka to tango, we follow the sound,
Wobbly rhythms, where smiles abound.

With instruments borrowed from junk in the street,
We tap on the pavement, our laughter is sweet,
The chorus of chaos is all we need here,
To welcome the moments, and wipe away fear.

So let's play our hearts out, with quirky delight,
In this joyful cacophony, everything's right,
For in this grand orchestra, life's not so bland,
In the symphony unscripted, we all take a stand.

Cartography of the Unexpected Journey

Maps of chaos line the walls,
With arrows pointing where the coffee stalls.
We sail on seas of spilled regrets,
And laugh at things we might forget.

A compass spins in dizzy loops,
As squirrels plot like clever troops.
We tread on paths of rubber ducks,
And dance with fate in woolly socks.

Directions? Who needs those today?
Let's twist and turn in our own way.
With every laugh, we skip a beat,
In this tasty mess, oh what a treat!

So grab a snack, it's time to roam,
The art of detours finds a home.
Each giggle marks the spots we roam,
In this grand jest that feels like home.

Building Castles on Shifting Ground

We strategize with marshmallow bricks,
As winds of change throw silly tricks.
Our towers wobble, our walls might sway,
Yet here we play, come what may.

Seagulls decree the royal decree,
'Hey, nothing's stable,' they squawk with glee.
We dance on floors of creamy pies,
In this grand hall of sweet alibis.

Our castles tremble, but spirits soar,
With laughter echoing through each door.
As tides rise high, we stand our ground,
In furry slippers, warmth we've found.

So let the winds blow, let them roar,
We'll build anew, and then explore.
Through sandy slips, our dreams are sown,
With smiles and giggles, we're not alone.

The Poetics of Unwritten Pages

With pens in hand, blank sheets await,
As search for plots that feel just great.
We scribble tales of zebras in hats,
On wild adventures with chatty cats.

Each page a canvas of silly schemes,
Of bubblegum castles and chocolate streams.
Characters dance in whims and whirls,
As laughter bubbles in cartoon swirls.

A story starts but takes its time,
With plot twists brewed in jumbled rhyme.
A dragon might just bake a pie,
We giggle as we wonder why.

So pen those lines, let ideas roam,
In this grand script, we find a home.
For stories unwritten might just be fun,
A quirky journey that's never done.

In the Web of What Could Be

We weave our dreams on silken threads,
In crazy patterns where logic treads.
A spider winks with a wink so sly,
As possibilities flutter by.

Dancing amid the webs we spin,
With every slip, we laugh and grin.
What if the moon is made of cheese?
Let's jump on clouds and do as we please.

The what-ifs swirl like a dizzy flame,
In this spaghetti of whimsical game.
We bounce from thoughts like popping corn,
In every moment, a new dawn is born.

So let your muse be wild and free,
In this grand web of what could be.
With joy we'll craft, with laughter we'll see,
The magic stitched in our jubilee.

Emblems of Fate

Woke up today, tripped on my shoe,
Thought I'd found wisdom, but just my breakfast too.
Round every corner, a mishap takes shape,
Maybe that's fortune, wearing a cape.

I asked for a sign, my luck took a nap,
Fate sent a bird, just to give me a flap.
It stole my sandwich; now I'm feeling quite sly,
Not sure if I'm clever or just really dry.

On paths filled with puddles, I leap and I land,
Each splash a reassurance, isn't this grand?
My umbrella's a hat, worn stubbornly wrong,
Yet somehow it feels like I belong.

In this dance with chaos, I swing and I sway,
With every misstep, I brighten the day.
So here's to the blunders, let's give them a cheer,
For in fumbling laughter, I'm glad I'm still here.

Portraits of Possibility

Staring at options like I'm at a buffet,
I'll take a little luck on the side, hey, hey!
But each time I bite, it's a wild surprise,
Like finding a pickle in my sweet potato pies.

Rolling dice in the game shops of fate,
I wonder if winning's just a matter of weight?
Will I trade my old jinx for some glitter and foam?
Or stick with my quirks that feel like home?

The colors keep changing as I brush on my fears,
Splat! A bright yellow – Oh! That's laughter, not tears.
Each stroke is a story, each shade holds a twist,
I giggle at chaos, a painter's true bliss.

So let's sketch out the future with silly surprise,
With hiccups of joy splashed across all our skies.
In portraits of maybes, let's wear our bright grins,
For laughter's the frame that holds us all in.

The Sway of the Universe

The cosmos is dancing, oh what a sight,
With stars doing salsa, everything feels right.
I watched them twirl, then stepped on my toes,
At least I have rhythm, or so it just goes.

An asteroid hops, two galaxies spin,
And here I am, mulling where to begin.
I asked for a comet, but it showed me a frog,
Guess cosmic creatures also love a good jog.

Gravity's pulling, but I'm ready to fly,
With my half-baked ideas, I'm reaching the sky.
I may stumble and laugh, it's a ride far from bland,
In the sway of the universe, I take my stand.

So toss me your stars, I'll throw in a joke,
Just keep the black holes far from my cloak.
Let's dance through the chaos, with joy, let's partake,
For in cosmic laughter, there's much to awake.

Footprints in the Sand

Walking through grains, I left quite a trail,
Each step full of giggles, with a side of fail.
I yelled to the tide, "Hey, don't wash them away!"
It answered with bubbles, a playful ballet.

Seagulls keep teasing, they swoop and they dive,
Stealing my snacks, making seagull jive.
The footprints are plenty, but where are my shoes?
Oh wait, they got washed - thanks, ocean blues!

Each tide brings adventure, wave after wave,
In this sandy mischief, I'm learning to brave.
I'll laugh at the laughter, and dance with the sand,
For in all of this chaos, the universe planned.

So here's to the footprints that wash out to sea,
Let's follow the laughter, just you and me.
With each little mishap, let's giggle and sing,
For in silly moments, we flourish, we spring.

www.ingramcontent.com/pod-product-compliance
Lightning Source LLC
Chambersburg PA
CBHW051644160426
43209CB00004B/779